ARCHANGELOLOGY
CAMAEL COURAGE

IF YOU CALL THEM THEY WILL COME

KIM CALDWELL

Archangelology LLC

A Division of Archangelology LLC

https://archangelology.com

Copyright © 2020 by Kim Caldwell

All rights reserved.

No part of this book may be reproduced in any form or by any electronic or mechanical means, including information storage and retrieval systems, without written permission from the author, except for the use of brief quotations in a book review.

This publication is designed to provide competent and reliable information regarding the subject matter covered. However, it is sold with the understanding that the author and publisher are not engaged in rendering medical and healthcare or any advice. Archangelology LLC, Together Publishing and all offerings are for entertainment purpose only. If you need medical, financial or any kind of help please consult a qualified professional.

Introduction Editing and enhancement Rachel Caldwell

Book Editing Grammarly

ISBN: 978-1-947284-37-1

Book Cover Picture Nicola Zalewski

Cover design Kim Caldwell

 Created with Vellum

1
ABOUT THE SERIES

"Logic will get you from point A to B. Imagination will take you everywhere."-- Einstein

This Archangelology book and the entire series aim to lift the reader one step at a time. You may read this piece anytime you desire Upliftment and want to feel good now, never underestimate the power of feeling good for creating more of what you want.

Choose this or any of the other Archangelology Books or Matching Audios to read or listen to for at least 44 nights and raise your vibration consistently for an Uplifted Feeling and Life.

This piece is one of a series of Angelic Upgrade books that fill you with Divine Angelic codes. Angelic laws are based on love and light and thus, operate for free-will, so we must call and ask the Archangels for help.

When working with your book relax, take deep breaths and ground to Mother Earth. Focus on Intentions for whatever it is your heart desires that are for the highest good of all involved. Intentions for these energies that we can not see but feel when we are ready. There are those that believe The Archangels are the Ones that make Law of Attraction Work.

This series of books take on a life of its own as the Archangels move and play from book to book, creating a Delicious Alchemy. Each book becomes an instrument in this Celestial Symphony for a more fulfilling life. Many of the Archangel books also carry and infuse the Violet Flame and Divine Connection to Mother Earth for a transformational experience.

Each book has a matching meditation audio available for your listening pleasure at https://archangelology.com. Please visit our site for your gifts. The book and the audio have similar wording, yet according to the Angels, they Upgrade us differently. Each medium has a unique experience, energetically Upgrading us in distinct ways. Each time you read or hear an Archangel Upgrade, a new dimension is added or adjusted for your benefit.

Become interactive with your book; when inspired, read the words aloud, and let them roll over you, feeling the love and magic that the Angels radiate. When inspired create your own rituals; there is no right or wrong way. As you play with the rock stars of the Celestial realm, you can expect your life to become more heavenly, more peaceful.

You may Notice Many Words are Uniquely Capitalized throughout this series; this is yet another way the Angels infuse us. When you see this try to feel that word or phrase; sensing the depth of its Intensity of Pure Divine Light throughout your Being.

The Archangel Energy is neither male

nor female. This gender fluidity is made clear in this series by the use of the word they or he/she speak to convey a non-gender energy that shifts roles to uplift and nurture you. The upgrades happen in Divine Time, and there is no schedule. There is no competition. There is no rush. Wherever you are in the process is perfect.

A word about the length of this book. "Less is more." This Series of books is the result of decades of study in the art of Law of Attraction, Angelic knowing and energy healing, condensed here for you in a format that will shift and benefit the reader. If you found your way here, you can expect miracles. As Einstein said, "There are only two ways to live your life. One is as though nothing is a miracle. The other is as though everything is a miracle." The matching audio to this book is 44 minutes, so working with that is always an option.

Both Neville Goddard and Albert Einstein stated that our imagination is the creative force. Goddard went so far as to imply that our imagination is the God/dess Energy. I mention this to you because as you read these words with much more than your eyes, let your imagination run wild with vivid pictures of the love the magical Archangels have for you and of your adventures together. Enjoy.

2
ABOUT ARCHANGEL CAMAEL

Archangel Camael is here to radiate courage in your life and help you feel safe and secure, which of course, is priceless. In life, sometimes it feels like we just won't be able to make it. In these times of hardship is when Archangel Camael can step in and empower us to move forward. Camael is a Divine Archangel who can bring infinite blessings and has unlimited abilities. One of Camael's specialties is her/his ability to help us clear the fear that keeps us from moving forward. Camael relinquishes pains and trauma, whether they are from the past, present, or future. Camael's ability to instill great courage in the face of trying times is an invaluable tool. She/He also infuses us with the Divine knowing of when to speak and when to sit back quietly letting the energy work itself out with no effort on our part for Divine interactions and outcomes.

St. Germain makes a special guest appearance to shimmer our lives with the Violet Flame for intense Divine healings and clearings. He works this Violet Flame on our behalf to clear harsh negative emotions so that we can have a peaceful state of mind and experience more bliss. St. Germain helps us to let go of feelings of unforgiveness, which blocks feelings of personal freedom. These sentiments are best understood when you experience them firsthand.

Camael teaches a full body chakra process to get your energies shimmering and feeling refreshed.

Archangels abide by the law of free will. They will not break or interfere with free will. Humans have free will for many reasons, among these being the importance of receiving Divine Lessons. So, if we need the help of magical wisdom knowledge, we ask the Archangels to help us, and they will come. Archangels can make good times great, and they can make hard times more bearable. They can bring Divine ideas and inspiration. They can even bring Divine Faith, Divine Courage, Divine Understanding, Divine Wisdom, and Divine Passion.

Spend some interactive time in this book, to reawaken your connection to a Celestial being that can make your life more Heavenly. Adapting these mindsets will help shift your consciousness and make you a magnet for confidence, peace, and prosperity in new refreshed ways. There is no right or wrong way to use this tool. All these Divinely Intelligent Angelic Upgrades happen with grace and ease at the individual's comfortable pace. The only thing I recommend you keep in the forefront of your practice is to ensure you are enjoying the process. Meet the Archangels in the Archangelology Book and Audio Series that are here to help you at this time. If you call on Camael, she/he will come, just as all of the Archangels will come to your assistance when beckoned. Spending time with Archangels creates a heavenly life. For gifts from the Archangels visit https://archangelology.com/home.

3

ARCHANGEL CAMAEL

Archangelology. Camael. Take a deep healing breath. We are now going on a journey with the beautiful Archangel Camael. Camael is a Divine Archangel that can do infinite things, has unlimited abilities. But some of Camael's specialties are her/his ability to help us clear fear. She/He has the capacity to help us get over any past hurts, pains, or traumas. Yes. And the ability to have great courage in the face of trying times that seem too much for us to handle. In life, sometimes it feels like we just won't be able to make it. This is when Archangel Camael can help us.

Now the beautiful, Divine Angels, Archangels, abide by the rule, the law of free will. They will not break or interfere with free will. Humans have free will for many reasons. Receiving Divine Lessons is part of it. So, the magical wisdom knowledge, once we understand it, is, if we call, if we ask the Archangels to help us, they will come. Archangels can make good times great, and they can make hard times more bearable. They can bring Divine Ideas. They can bring Divine Faith, Divine Courage, Divine Understanding, Divine Wisdom, Divine Passion.

Close your eyes and raise your hand, and repeat after me when you are ready. "Archangel Camael, please come into my life now, and help me. Give me strength. Give me courage. Help me clear my past fears, my fears now. Help me forgive. Help me clear any blocks that are holding me back. Help me release anything that is keeping me from my highest good. Archangel Camael, help me now. Thank you." Deep healing breath.

Now, please look up and see a beautiful,

beautiful panoramic screen. Yes. Look up on that screen, and see the beautiful, Divine Archangel Camael standing there in front of you in all of her/his glory. Angels are neither male or female. They are the infusion of male energies with the female energies, with the Divine Energies. They are such a lovely, lovely blend, the Archangels and Angels are. They infuse us with so much Divine Love and Divine Knowing. They help us when we are ready to come into our God/dess self. They are God/desses, beautiful, beautiful messengers to help us, to give us faith and courage. Deep healing breath.

As you stand before the beautiful Archangel, She/he is shining such light to you. She/He is shining such light on you. Now, Camael is going to help you balance your base chakra. That is our chakra for survival. And as we work with this chakra and become aware of, blend, and balance this chakra, we're going to start to feel more safe, more secure, more balanced. This chakra is red. I want you to see the chakra, and I want you to see it like a spinning wheel spinning right at the base of your genital area. Now see it spinning and then let it stop. Take a deep breath and watch it spin again. Spinning, spinning clockwise. Let out your air. See it spinning, watch it spinning. It's lying flat. It is a circle, and it spins, and then it can stop. As it spins, it creates a rush of energy that goes up your spine. Beautiful. See it spin, watch it stop. Deep healing breath.

Camael's watching. Now, watch as Camael shimmers beautiful, beautiful sparkles at that area as your chakra spins and balances and cleanses and clears. Camael looks at you with the sweetest, kindest eyes you've ever seen and gives you the telepathic message that she/he is going to clean and clear and heal this chakra for you now. Anytime you need, you feel afraid, or you have fear, Camael will help you by doing this exercise with you. Now watch as his finger points and your chakra spins and energy bursts up. Up, up, up your whole chakra system. Your whole spine. Take a deep breath.

Now watch as that beautiful energy rushes up to the next chakra. Right in between your belly button and your genital area. This is your sacral chakra. Now, Archangel Camael points to your sacral chakra. Watch that chakra spin like a pinwheel as energy shoots up it and then glows and stops. Deep healing breath. Spin orange shimmers of light like a pinwheel again, healing this chakra. This process is giving you confidence and balance with your sacral chakra. Spin orange and watch the orange shimmers of light, so healing and beautiful to your sacral chakra. Just moving that energy and healing you and clearing you on deep levels. Yes.

Now, the energy moves up again to your naval chakra. Your naval chakra is spinning, spinning, spinning. See a spinning, flat circle orb spinning. Deep healing breath. See it spin like a pinwheel. Spin and then stop. Spin and then stop. This chakra is a beautiful golden-yellow color. Deep healing breath as you spin the chakra, then stop. Spin then stop. Now, Archangel Camael points to that chakra for you, infusing you with well-being, with deep self-love, with the knowing of how the angels adore and love you on deep, deep levels. Deep healing breath. Yes. Feel all that

Divine Love flowing to you now. Camael smiles at you gently as she/he just pours Divine Love into this area, letting you know that everything is okay. It always has been okay. It always will be okay.

As she/he does this to your naval area, you feel lighter and lighter. You feel the stresses of the world melting away, and you feel as though you can do anything. Deep healing breath. Camael wants you to know she's/he's cleansing and healing this area, and as she does, any of your past traumas are just disappearing. Now, at this Solar Plexus area, I want you to see this area glowing like a Sun, glowing like a Sun. And I want you to see a line going all the way to the left, all the way out through eternity, and all the way to the right, going all the way out to eternity, and it's an inter-dimensional timeline. It is your personal timeline. And Camael is just going to Infuse that chakra, that sacral energy that is glowing like a Sun now. There's a Sun now. Camael is going to direct that Sun, that beautiful little, personal Sun, just to open up, and all the energy to move all the way to the past, all your past, and then the other side to move all the way to the future.

Now what Archangel Camael is doing at this moment is clearing all your past and present hurts, all your past and present situations that are stuck there. Take a deep healing breath. Feel that love. Know that you are so Divinely Supported and Loved. See this happening now, as that beautiful, Divine Sun clears and heals the past trauma. Watch it shimmer. Know that this Father Sun, your personal Sun, is doing all the work for you as Camael supports you and loves you and directs you. As this chakra is cleansed, cleared, healed, filled with light and love, you feel as if you could fly. As your confidence and your knowing upgrades. Deep healing breath.

Now, the Sun starts to come back, all refreshed and clean, back to your belly button chakra, and spin there. And you watch it as it spins, a beautiful, beautiful golden light. Take a deep healing breath. You are refreshed. You feel bright. You feel ready for that energy to move to the next chakra, your beautiful, glowing, green heart chakra.

Take a deep healing breath. Camael helps to direct that energy straight up to your heart chakra. As your chakra spins, spins flat like a pinwheel, your heart opens and clears. Spins and then stops. Spins and then stops. This is how Camael cleans and heals your chakras. The energy spins in that heart area. And as Camael spins this energy in your heart area, he reminds you that now is the time that you choose to remember to move your thinking mechanism into your heart. Your goal is to think with your heart instead of your head. We aspire to become a heart-centered human again. To come back and be an earth-angel. Deep healing breath.

Now watch as that gorgeous, gorgeous Archangel Camael spins all the beautiful green energy, the shimmers, the shimmering light, the beautiful shimmering light right into your heart chakra. Notice how light and peaceful you feel. How you feel like you're floating as you close your eyes, look up at the screen, and watch as Camael does this for you. All of a sudden, you see hundreds of little fairies all around you, stringing love to you, circling you, filling with love, filling you with divine love, filling you with peaceful, divine light, filling you with radiance. These are your personal fairies. They love to bring you feelings of security and to give you wonderful ideas. They love to help you let go of things from the past. They love to clear fears.

These are such special little fairies, and you're re-acquainting yourself with them now. Deep healing breath. You can hear the little fairy songs and their little beautiful, beautiful voices shimmering in your ears, shimmering in your heart. And as you look up on the screen in your mind's eye, it looks like beautiful small orbs of light all around you in a circle. You look so beautiful. So many beautiful, beautiful fairies in so many beautiful colors and beautiful orbs of light and flashes of light. You start just to relax and smile and enjoy the beautiful show as Archangel Camael, and his fairies heal your heart.

Heal your heart from past pain, from past sorrow, from past trauma. This can be from past lives. We've had many, many traumas in past lives. This causes many humans to shut down their hearts. To close off, to create heart walls. Archangel Camael wants you to know it's safe now. It's safe now to open your heart to love. Ask Archangel Camael now with me. Deep healing breath. "Archangel Camael, please guide me to benevolent beings, to benevolent people in my life that I can trust with my heart. Like minds. These people are soulmates of a sort. Beings I can trust, be myself around, enjoy, people who can have fun with me. Yes. Archangel Camael, guide me with divine wisdom to find the best, most bright, most beautiful souls who I enjoy and who enjoy me. Archangel Camael, let me know I am safe now. Let me know that everything's okay and that I can open my heart to love again. That I don't have to be afraid anymore."

Archangel Camael hears your request and sends such deep love into your eyes and lets you know that she/he is with you now, one of your protectors. Camael represents the energy of the planet Mars. Strength. Courage. And you have a strong, gorgeous Archangel in your corner now, who any time you call upon is there for you and will help you. Deep healing breath. Now, Archangel Camael helps to direct that energy and move it up quickly. Move it up to the throat chakra. Deep healing breath, and watch like a pinwheel as it spins and stops. Spins, that throat chakra spins, and stops. You're activating it; you're healing it, you're cleansing it. Archangel Camael is doing all the work; you're just watching on the screen as he does. Archangel Camael balances your beautiful chakras.

Now, Archangel Camael works on your throat chakra. Cleaning, the beautiful, bright, blue light as your throat chakra spins and stops. Feel the activation of that chakra. Feel the energy coming alive. Feel as the blue sparkles go out, shimmering. Feel as Archangel Michael heals your chakra, your throat chakra, and fills it with love and light and peace and happiness. Archangel Camael lets you now that you are safe now to speak your truth. She knows that in other times when you spoke your truth, possibly traumas happened, possibly hard things happened. You are safe now. You will know when you can speak your truth, and you will speak it.

When you're not in the best of circumstances, you will relax and use your divine wisdom from the angels and sit back and watch. Sometimes the smartest thing we can say is nothing. Deep healing breath.

Now, Archangel Camael helps to blow the energy up to the third eye. Move it up very quickly, like wind going through the pinwheel. And it spins and stops. Deep healing breath. See that energy again, spinning and stop. Spin and stop. Yes. Camael is cleaning and clearing this energy again. Deep healing breath. It's radiating a beautiful violet, right at your third eye and you just watch, and you can see as Camael puts her beautiful finger to your forehead at your third eye and it just radiates and shimmers. You feel all the beautiful, shimmering violet energy shimmering there now. Deep healing breath.

As Archangel Camael does this, a beautiful, beautiful special guest is coming and wants to appear. It is the beautiful, beautiful Saint Germain. Saint Germain is the keeper of the violet flame. We may call the violet flame any time we need in our lives to help to clear out and cleanse anything. Anything that no longer serves us. Deep healing breath. Now, as you stand, up on the screen you can see yourself. You're like a movie star. You're so beautiful. You're so handsome. You're so handsome. You're so perfect. You're so attractive. And you look, and you watch on the movie screen, and there you are, standing there, in a beautiful, green, lush field with Archangel Camael standing beside you and the beautiful, beautiful Saint Germain on your other side. Saint Germain wants you to know that any time you need, when you're having harsh thoughts, you can take the beautiful violet flame right in your third eye and watch that cooling, soothing violet flame shimmer and melt away anything that no longer serves you.

See that with your third eye. See the beautiful, beautiful violet flame. See it shimmering, see it melting away any heavy thoughts, any fears, any unforgiveness that might be there, that might be blocking us. See that beautiful violet flame just helping to release any of that. Any of those thoughts, any of those blocks, anything that no longer serves us. As you do this, as you stand there, like the brave, courageous soul that you are, Archangel Camael places his hands around your head, and you feel this beautiful tingling, tingling, and this beautiful light is emanating from these two divine beings right onto you. Deep healing breath. They're at this moment, healing you of all fear, healing you of any blocks, healing you of any unforgiveness, healing you of any judgments you've held against yourself, or judgment you've held of others.

What we're doing here is very divine work. What you're doing is so courageous and so wonderful. Camael wants you to know how beautifully proud she is of you. Deep healing breath. As you stand there, and these divine, divine beings work on you, you start to feel so light. You feel as if your whole body is gently lifting off the ground. And yes, you're lifting, and the beautiful masters are lifting with you. And then you see another divine being walking up to you. He is a divine being of love. You smile because you recognize this gorgeous, gorgeous being, and it's Jesus. Because, what better teacher to come, what better master, Jesus our brother, our divine enlightened master, who went before us and now is helping to show us the way to our mastery. What better divine master to show us how to forgive? How to move forward into our divinity when things happen that feel so hard and so wrong to us. Deep healing breath.

Now as you stand there, you're in awe as you watch as Jesus smiles at you, and you see his whole heart area glowing with bright, divine light. That white, divine light starts shimmering. Rays and rays of light are coming from Jesus, and it's engulfing you. It feels so Divine and so good and so beautiful. It feels like the warmest, kindest, most celestial love, you've every experienced. Deep healing breath. Just continue to feel these waves of love flowing over you, washing you, healing you, filling you with every bit of divine, angelic, majestic, masterful love in the universe. You feel so good you can't even think, you just lay back and float as Jesus continues to fill you with his divine, white light.

Now, Archangel Camael walks on the

other side of you and places her hands right underneath your back, your shoulders, and one on your lower back, as divine support. Archangel Camael wants you to know that you're always supported, even when things feels hard and times feel tough; you are supported, you are loved. Deep healing breath. Feel the love and the support radiating through you now as Archangel Camael holds you in this divine, floating, comfortable position. Now, Saint Germain moves to where your head is. As you lay there and float, Saint Germain puts his hands right at the base of your neck. Oh, right there where it always feels a little tense. Now Saint-Germain starts infusing that whole area with a violet flame. As he does this, he sends you the telepathic message to completely relax as he goes in with his divine violet flame and releases any plugs, any tensions. Yes. Deep healing breath.

You can just feel it all melting and popping away. All the stress, all the tension. Yes, all at the same time. Archangel Camael holds you, support you, warms your back. Yes, while at the same time Jesus floods your heart with sweet, white, love and light. You are at this moment in pure, divine ecstasy. Deep healing breath as you float and you hear the beautiful choir of your angels singing just for you. Singing songs of love, singing songs of hope, giving you energetic downloads of healing, cleansing, filling you with courage. At this moment, you know that you're being recharged and renewed to experience a brand new you. You understand now that everything that you went through, every hardship, every trial, made you the amazing, powerful, creator that you are today. Deep healing breath.

You feel this power coursing through you, and you know, you know that now, anytime you need, you simply ask your beautiful divine Camael to walk with you. Camael can walk beside you or in front of you or behind you. It makes no difference. He just wants you to feel safe and guided and protected and to know what a perfect, gorgeous being you are and how proud he is to stand by your side at any moment in time.

Now, see yourself again, upon the beautiful, panoramic screen. And Archangel

Camael is going to work with a very special healing [toll 00:34:21] for you. Archangel Camael stands you right in front of him and stands back a bit. Camael is going to put an energetic Taurus at the base of your spine. A Taurus looks like a donut, and the energy swirls and circles all around. So it's swirling around you circles and circles and circles, and it cleans and clears. This energetic Taurus at your base chakra, the chakra that gives you stability and makes you feel safe, is going to spin with a beautiful, sparkling, coppery-red color. Yes, watch it as it spins. Deep healing breath. As this is happening, your whole body feels invigorated. You are being given an infusion. An infusion of courage, and will, and strength, and of knowing.

This Taurus energy, this copper, shimmering, metallic energy is infusing you with a renewal of spirit. You feel a renewal of life as you listen to the angels sing. Your Taurus spins and balances you. As this happens, Archangel Camael lets you know that all your ancestors of the past are at this moment with you. Being cleared and being healed of all trauma, of all fear. Archangel Camael is going back as far as is. Also, Archangel Camael is helping to clear you on dimensions. Deep healing breath.

Now Camael is moving the energy forward in time. Yes. Clearing the path for you so that as challenges happen, you will have the strength and renewed knowing that everything is okay and divine and that your benevolent beings, your Archangels, your angels, you fairies, your masters, your guides are with you always. These Divine beings are supporting and loving you. It is done. All the trauma of the past cleared. All the fear of the past is cleared, and you're infused with divine courage. And you're surrounded by a team of knights. You can see these knights. You are their king or queen. They guard you. They protect you. You're being introduced to beautiful, beautiful knights. See them; see them in their glory. Watch them as they turn to your highness. They would give their lives for you. They love you and adore you.

Each knight has a different job. You delegate these jobs to these knights. One knight is in charge of protecting you. One knight is in charge of collecting abundance for you. One knight is in charge of divine love for you, helping you to find divine love. One knight is in charge of health. Yes, these knights surround you. You are their king/queen. You are the reason they exist, to make you happy, to make things better for you, and to make your life easier. Connect with them now. Take a deep, healing breath. You will cultivate a relationship with them. You will see them more often. You will call upon them, now that you know they're there. And they report to Archangel Camael. Camael is the strong Archangel of Mars, of courage, who lives to protect and take care of you.

Now, as your heart swells, and you wonder what you've done to deserve such love, such protection, such kindness, Archangel Camael telepathically sends you the message that you are the most beautiful child of the god/goddess. That you are the king/queen, prince/princess of your kingdom, and that she wants you to spend more time with her in meditation so that you may enjoy this kingdom that you are rediscovering and creating now, where you are so brave and so courageous and you can accomplish anything. Your kingdom is where benevolent forces work 24 hours a day, seven days a week to make you happy. Yes. Come here often with Archangel Camael and your beautiful knights and to your beautiful, sparkling kingdom. See your kingdom sparkling. It looks like a fairy tale. It looks so beautiful. You can see it floating, like a dream, like a city of light. It is yours. You created it, and now you see it again.

Now, this is the world that is etheric. It's being created; it's already created on the etheric level. And you create this etheric world with your imagination because of Neville Goddard, one of my favorite master teachers, who explained that imagination is the god/goddess force. So, as we create this etheric world that is real on the etheric level, it moves out into our lives. It branches out and makes our kingdom that much more wonderful. It makes our lives a divine game. It makes our lives more fun, and we can pull in all of the benevolent characters that we wish were on our side, who support us with divine love. Archangels support you with divine peace and want you to have divine joy, bliss, and abundance. They want your life to sparkle with all of the abundance that you can imagine and more.

This is your beautiful kingdom. Who, more than you, deserves it? This kingdom is your secret. As your kingdom is your secret, you can create amazing levels. Yes. Keep this beautiful, etheric kingdom secret, and let all the benevolent light-beings and archangels help you make it everything that your heart ever desired and more. Yes. Take a deep, healing breath. You are the queen or king. You are the god or goddess, and you are surrounded by archangels, light-beings, and all the benevolent help you can imagine. You are divine.

Say it with me now: "I am divine. I am safe. I am courageous. I am creating on incredible new levels now. I am that I am." Take a deep, healing breath. "Archangel Camael, thank you."

4

ANGELIC MANIFESTATION JOURNAL BONUS

Writing down your Blessings with Archangel Barachiel on a daily or consistent basis is going to enhance your world. There has never been a better time to Focus on your Blessings with this Power.

Create more of the life you want with the Archangels as you explore and Focus with your Angelic Journal. If you are ready, let's set intentions now to make your Archangel Barachiel Book a Manifestation tool. It is said that humans have so many thoughts going on in our heads at once that it is hard for Angels and Spirit Guides to hear what we want help with. This is one of the many reasons it is so powerful to get very clear on what we desire and write it out in a designated journal for our Archangels. This way, they can understand our needs better and help us with our dreams and goals in Divine Time.

It has been proven that when we write things down, more of what we desire comes to us. Goals get accomplished, and things flow with more ease. Adding the Amazing Archangels to your journaling just makes the results that much stronger. As we set intentions for what we want and take the time to focus and write it down in our journal, unseen forces move on our behalf. We are going to enlist the help of this Divine Knowing with our Archangel book in an interactive way and turn our book into a manifestation tool. We are also going to play with our books like children and have some fun. Children are powerful creators, and we will take on some of their great habits for their creative value.

Focus and underline ideas you resonate with in your book and become immersed in Upliftment. There is a deeper connection as we become interactive with our Archangel books. We may get colored pens and underline areas of our book that feel important or special to us. We may want to draw pictures of desired blessings or anything that makes us feel good. We may want to mark different areas of our book with hearts, stars, or Angel wings. Get sticky tab notes, a personal favorite, and stick them to your favorite pages you want to return to often. In your journal section, place a sticky tab on an area you want to let the Angels know to help you write in and as a personal reminder. Let your Angelic interaction and intuition guide you with what feels best. Neville Goddard and Albert Einstein both explained that our imagination is a creative force and can bring great blessings to our lives. We will bring our imagination fully into our process now. You may want to add stickers to enhance pages. Place a beautiful angel or magic looking card in your book as a bookmark. Get creative and give your book some personal character. Putting clover or flowers in your book to press and dry, adds some powerful nature magic to your process. Roses are a great choice as they have the highest vibration of any flower. You may give lovely flowers as an offering to your Archangels as well. Giving back is always a beneficial activity.

Everyone has magical abilities. Some of us know this, and some do not. My point is all these ideas are simple and will work for anyone who puts forth an effort and has the faith to relax and let go so the Angels may do their work. Of course, anything we put out comes back to us, so we want to always include "for the highest good" in all requests.

In all my studies of magical herbs, cinnamon is found in many different traditions for enhancement of all things wanted and removing things not wanted. You may want to rub a dab of cinnamon mixed with a touch of olive oil on your journal in an intentional shape such as a heart for more love or the infinity symbol for more abundance. Then say to yourself, "I anoint my journal with success and happiness with the help of the Archangels." Anointment has been practiced for eons with much luck and advancement. Basil and Sage could just as easily be utilized. Anything that feels magical and speaks to you in your spice cabinet most likely has wonderful magical properties. Use these gifts of nature with intention and focus for a more joyous life. The idea is to create a magnet for all you desire that is for your highest good with your Archangel Journal.

You may want to underline ideas in colors that mean something to you. The sky is the limit, get creative and juicy with your book, knowing that amazing things are being created.

Next, we have dedicated pages that are waiting for you to fill them with your heart's desires that Barahciel will help you achieve as long as they are for the highest good. You may write anything you want in your Archangel Journal. There is no right or wrong way to do this. You may ask the Archangels to help you release things from your life, share your hopes and dreams, or ask questions. I ask my angels questions, patiently wait, and know they will lead me to the answer in Divine Time.

Be open and honest with your journaling and the Archangels understanding that the only ones who need to see your Angel Journal are you and your Angels. Keeping your wishes to yourself is very powerful for manifesting as well.

We have created categories for you, and of course, there will Be freestyle areas, so play with this and have fun. After you play with your journal, you may put it away in a sacred space knowing all is in Divine Order. Remember, magic works just in its own time and asking where the results are will only block things, so relax, have faith, and patience. Keep this dream book; you will be pleasantly surprised when you check on it at later dates. You may come back to read your Archangel book and add more to it at any time. Know that unseen beneficial forces are moving to help you now and forevermore. Play with and collect other Archangelology books and audios, remembering, "If you call them, they will come." Check out the Archangelology Archangel Journaling Book for more ideas on taking your Journaling Process to the next "celestial" level. The Archangels have tied this whole series Together for us in such a Divinely Intelligent way. Spend time in nature with your book, filling it with love, imagination, and Angelic magic for exponential results. You are a powerful creator and loved by all that is.

Write on the blank areas of your book and on the lined journal areas. Think outside of the box and let your kid like creative energies flow. Have fun, and add your own flair.

Please enjoy the process and expect wonderful things.

5

CONFIDENCE JOURNALING

Write out all the Confidence you feel with this Courageous Archangel by your side. See Cinnamon Light blessings all in your Energy Field. Write, I Am Confident, and Archangel Camael stands by my side anytime I call them.

6

COURAGE TAP WITH ARCHANGEL CAMAEL

Tap the center of your chest and say aloud to yourself I am filled with courage as Archangel Camael stands with me now. Write about different ways you would like to invite Archangel Camael into your life for more Confidence and to know what a powerful creator you are with all the Archangel's support.

FINDING YOUR COURAGE MAGIC

Write an Imagination Creation of how Archangel Camael's support and encouragement feel to you. Hint: It has an air of happiness knowing you can do anything you want. Allow all your dreams, Love, Vitality, and Confidence to flow in your Journal. And get creative and draw your Powerful Angel wings.

7

COURAGE WITH CAMAEL

Visualize Archangel Camael around you, moving their Angel Wings through your energetic body, removing anything that no longer serves you. Allow them to remove any feelings of fear that humans sometimes experience. As Archangel Camael creates beautiful spaces in your field, ask them to fill them with Courage, Faith, Confidence, and more. Write all the incredible energies you are experiencing.

8

CAMAEL AND ST. MARTHA BOOSTER

St. Martha is a super protective Saint who helps you create healthy, energetic boundaries.

Archangel Camael is a master at boosting courage and Confidence. These two Masters work together to help you learn more about energetic boundaries and help you implement them. Write places you would like Divine assistance with this.

ARCHANGEL CAMAEL BLESSINGS

Feel as Archangel Camael and St. Martha stand around you with the Moon Angels in a circle. Feel the Violet Flame surround you as you take relaxing breaths. Feel Angelic peace and security infuse you. Call this good energy into your life and the ones you love. Write how this can assist you and your entire circle of influence.

9

ARCHANGEL CAMAEL AND ST. RITA

Saint Rita is a beautiful Saint for helping people get seemingly impossible wishes. She is a divine blessing to those who call on her.

Archangel Camael is known for helping people develop more courage. Write how these benevolent beings can help you gain more faith, patience, and courage and call in Divine Wishes for the highest good. Try to let go of expectations and allow what the Divine Beings bring. Write some of your wishes for fun.

CALL ON ARCHANGEL CAMAELS STRENGTH

Call Archangel Camael to remove the weight of the world off your shoulders. Visualize as Archangel Camael lifts burdens and feel the tingling lightness in your imagination. Take a deep breath and sigh. Allow your imagination to ignite all the fabulous possibilities. Write in your Journal about what you would like Archangel Camael to lift. Write how different things feel with your Archangel's help.

10

ARCHANGEL CAMAEL WISHES

Ask St. Rita to help you remember a moment when you felt pleased. If you can not think of one, ask St. Rita to help you create an incredible feeling of wishes granted and your life feeling great in your imagination. Allow this feeling to enhance you and bask in it for as long as possible. Feel as Archangel Camael holds your hand and helps you continue this feeling. See golden sparkles of wishes fulfilled all around you. Write about how great this feels. Neville Goddard says, "It is the feeling place that creates."

ARCHANGEL CAMAEL
VIBE LIFT

Call Archangel Camael and St. Rita to stand around you. Feel brilliant sparkles of red light dance around the three of you. Smile as you raise your vibration with your Saint and Archangel. Ask St. Rita and Archangel Camael to help you regularly cultivate the feeling of your wishes being fulfilled. Write a few things you love about your Confidence regularly. Smile and lift.

ARCHANGEL CAMAEL
SUPERHERO

Write out all the different little ways you feel confident in your life. Add a list of things you want to be more courageous with, and ask Archangel Camael to help you. Write out how you move when you feel in your Power. Get creative with this and bring your superhero energy from your childhood to your journaling. Have fun with your Archangels.

11

CREATIVE JOURNALING FOR A BLESSED LIFE

Fill these pages with any creative ideas that you desire your Archangels to help you line Up. Have fun. Get out your colored pens. Draw hearts filled with Violet Flame, beautiful landscapes, flowers, and anything that makes you smile.

ARCHANGEL CAMAEL
SPARKLING CONFIDENCE

Fill your Journal with colorful drawings, symbols, and sacred geometry that attracts. Allow Archangel Camael to help you fill the pages with Sparkling Confidence.

12

JOURNALING FOR NEW BLESSINGS

Ideas for New Blessings my Archangels help me bring to Life for the highest good. Let this evolve and grow for the highest good.

I AM FOCUSED ON MY CONFIDENCE

Faith is the art of seeing the unseen. Ask Archangel Camael for help visualizing and playing with your imagination. Focus on all your Sparkling Blessings. Feel them floating around you and bring this to the page.

13

JOURNALING YOUR GRATITUDE

Fill these pages with the things you appreciate. Feel how abundantly blessed you are. The eyes to read this is cause for celebration.

ARCHANGEL CAMAEL FOR MORE SELF LOVE

Call in Archangel Camael and ask them how they can bring more courage to your relationship with yourself and more courage to be yourself. Feel Archangel Camael shimmer Angelic Red Sparkles around your heart center. These shimmers clear any pain and old resentments away. Feel as your heart makes way for more self-love. List different ideas for courage and more self-love.

DANCE AND PLAY WITH ARCHANGEL CAMAEL

Write about all the fun you and Archangel Camael can have in your imagination, such as dancing and playing. Feeling like a rock star from the celestial field is your friend and great support. Write out all the fun things you see yourself doing. Get creative and play with your Archangels.

14

PAMPER YOURSELF WITH ARCHANGEL CAMAEL

Make a list of ways you can pamper yourself and add to it. Ask Archangel Camael for guidance and support on putting yourself first and creating healthy boundaries. Write any ideas you get and add them regularly.

15

WRITE IT OUT

Accepting and making Peace with where we are is hugely helpful. In life, when things come up, that feel we have no control, a great tool is to "write it out." We will do this to write out all the anger, hurt and stressful feelings for "letting it go." As we let it go, we create space for more Peace. For this exercise, get a separate piece of paper that you will tear up once you finish writing out all the hurt and anger. This paper is for your eyes only, so say all the things you need to speak to the person or situation and do not hold back. Get it all out. Write and write till you feel a sigh of relief. This can take as long as you need. Once you finish, you will tear the paper up and throw it away, or you may burn it in a safe place. Either way, the intention here is to let it go. If you need to do this process for more than one day, keep it up till you feel better. May this bring you Peace and Blessings or something better. Again, do not show this to anyone. This is for your relief and energetic shift. As you feel better, your world will too.

16

BLESSINGS

May the Divine Creative Force that Moves and Creates the Universes Bless and Enhance Every Wish You Ever Conceived that is for the Highest Good of All Involved. May Joy, Peace, and Purpose Be Yours all the Days of your Lives. Through All Time Space and Dimensions. So Mote it Be, and So It Is. I hope this book helps you in wonderful ways and radiates out to a gorgeous future for you and yours.

Kim

REFERENCES

Chaudhary Sufian. World of Archangels: How to Meet an Archangel. (Sufian Chaudhary 2012).

Damon Brand. The 72 Angels of Magick. (Damon Brand).

Esther and Jerry Hicks. The Essential Law of Attraction Collection. (Hay House).

James Mangan. The Secret of Perfect Living. (James Mangan)

Matias Flury. Downloads From The Nine: Awaken As You Read. (Matias Flury 2014)

Og Mandino. The God Memorandum. (Fell Publishers 1995).

17

MORE OFFERINGS

Visit https://archangelology.com to discover more Archangels and Super Power Saints

Each of the following books has a matching audio filled with healing music.

Archangelology Michael * Protection

Archangelology Raphael * Abundance

Archangelology Camael * Courage

Archangelology Gabriel * Hope

Archangelology Metatron * Well Being

Archangelology Uriel * Peace

Archangelology Haniel * Love

Archangelology Raziel * Wisdom

Archangelology Zadkiel * Forgiveness

Archangelology Jophiel * Glow

Archangelology Violet Flame * Oneness

Archangelology Sun Angels * Power

Archangelology Moon Angels * Magnetism

Archangelology Sandalphon * Harmony

Archangelology Orion * Expansion

The items below come in book only

Archangelology * Archangel Journaling

Archangelology * Archangel Breath-Tap Book

How Green Smoothies Saved My Life Book

Activate Your Abundance Book and Audio Program

The rest of the items below are available in Audio Format

Archangelology*Mary Magdalene*Feminine Divine Audio

Archangelology * Breath-Tap Super Power Saints Volume 1 Audio

Archangelology * Breath-Tap Super Power Saints Volume 2 Audio

Regeneration Meditations * Switchword Series with Solfeggio Frequencies audio

Radiating Divine Love * Switchword Series with Solfeggio Frequencies audio

Love Charm * Switchword Series with Solfeggio Frequencies audio

Dragon Sun Grounding Meditations * Cosmic Consciousness Series audios

Sweet Moon Sleep Meditation * Cosmic Consciousness Series

Enchanted Earth Sacred Geometry * Cosmic Consciousness Series audios

18

PLEASE WRITE A HELPFUL REVIEW.

If you enjoyed Barachiel please give this Book a positive review so others may find it as well. And may blessings come back for your help.

Thank you so much.

Kim

www.ingramcontent.com/pod-product-compliance
Lightning Source LLC
Chambersburg PA
CBHW060416090426
42734CB00011B/2339